OPEN YOUR BUSINESS:

A Step-by-Step Guide to Starting and Growing a Successful Enterprise

Norris Elliott

ELLIONAIRE BOOKS

Copyright © 2023 Norris Elliott

All rights reserved

The characters and events portrayed in this book are fictitious. Any similarity to real persons, living or dead, is coincidental and not intended by the author.

No part of this book may be reproduced, or stored in a retrieval system, or transmitted in any form or by any means, electronic, mechanical, photocopying, recording, or otherwise, without express written permission of the publisher.

ISBN-13:

Cover design by: Norris Elliott
Library of Congress Control Number:
Printed in the United States of America

This handbook is dedicated to all entrepreneurs with the courage and determination to chase their dreams. Starting and growing a business is a challenging journey, and we understand the effort, dedication, and sacrifice it takes to turn an idea into a successful enterprise. This handbook is for all the entrepreneurs who dare to take the first step and have the determination to see it through. It's for all the entrepreneurs who work tirelessly to turn their vision into reality and never give up on their dreams. We admire and respect your determination, hard work, and perseverance. This handbook is a small token of our appreciation for all you do, and we hope it will be a valuable resource as you continue on your entrepreneurial journey. This book is dedicated to all the entrepreneurs out there who are working hard to make their dreams come true.

"Your work will fill a large part of your life, and the only way to be truly satisfied is to do what you believe is great work. And the only way to do great work is to love what you do. If you haven't found it yet, keep looking. Don't settle. As with all matters of the heart, you'll know when you find it." -

STEVE JOBS.

FOREWORD

Starting a business is one of an individual's most challenging and rewarding experiences. It requires a combination of passion, skill, and determination to turn an idea into a successful enterprise. As an entrepreneur, you will face several challenges, from raising capital and building a team to creating a viable product or service and developing a solid brand.

This handbook is designed to help entrepreneurs navigate the complex process of starting and growing a business. It covers various topics, from creating a business plan and obtaining funding to managing finances, marketing and sales, and building and maintaining a solid team. It Also covers legal and compliance, financing and accounting, organizational behavior, sales and promotion, productivity, risk management, networking, building relationships, and environmental and social sustainability.

The handbook also includes tips and strategies for attracting and retaining employees and motivating and engaging your team.

The information in this handbook is based on the latest research and best practices in entrepreneurship. It is designed to give entrepreneurs the knowledge and tools they need to start and grow their businesses.

This handbook will be a valuable resource for entrepreneurs as they embark on starting and growing their businesses. Whether you are a first-time entrepreneur or an experienced business owner, the information in this handbook will be of great value to you.

The book is organized into chapters, each covering a specific topic. Each chapter includes tips, strategies, and examples to help entrepreneurs understand and apply the information to their businesses.

Let's get started on your journey to open your business. We wish you all the best as you embark on your entrepreneurial journey. May your business be successful!

PREFACE

Starting a business is a dream for many people, but it can also be daunting and overwhelming. There are countless questions to consider, from crafting a business plan and obtaining funding to building a team and marketing your product or service. It's important to clearly understand the key concepts and strategies essential for starting and growing a successful business.

Throughout the handbook, we provide practical tips and strategies that entrepreneurs can use to start and grow their businesses. We also include case studies and examples of real-world companies to illustrate key concepts and techniques.

We encourage entrepreneurs to seek additional resources and guidance as they open and grow their businesses. This handbook is not meant to be a substitute for professional advice but a starting point for entrepreneurs looking to spread and grow their businesses.

BUSINESS PLANNING

A business plan is a document that outlines a business's goals, strategies, and operational objectives. It serves as a roadmap for the company and is used to guide decision-making and measure progress. A well-written business plan is essential for the success of any business, as it helps entrepreneurs to identify and evaluate opportunities, set realistic goals, and secure financing.

Critical components of a business plan include:

- Executive summary: A brief overview of the business, its products or services, target market, and financial projections.
- Business Description: A detailed business description, including its history, mission, and vision.
- Industry analysis: A review of the industry in which the business operates, including market size, growth prospects, and trends.

- Market analysis: A description of the target market, including demographics, buying habits, and competition.
- Product or service line: A description of the business's products or services, including unique features and benefits.
- Marketing and sales strategies: A description of how the business will reach and sell to its target market.
- Operations plan: A description of how the business will operate, including the location, equipment, and personnel required.
- Financial plan: A projection of the financial performance of the business, including income statements, cash flow statements, and balance sheets.

Tips for using the business plan to guide decision-making and measure progress:

- Review the business plan regularly and update it as needed.
- Use the financial projections in the business plan to set financial goals and track progress.
- Use the strategies outlined in the project as a guide for decision-making.
- Use market and industry analysis to identify and evaluate growth opportunities.
- Use the operations plan to identify and address operational issues.

Creating a business plan can take time and effort, but it is crucial to starting and running a successful business. Entrepreneurs should take the time to research and gather information, seek input from others, and carefully consider their options before finalizing their plans.

In this chapter, we have covered the importance of having a business plan, critical components, and tips on using a business plan to guide decision-making and measure progress. The next chapter will delve into starting a business's legal and compliance aspects.

LEGAL AND COMPLIANCE

Starting and running a business involves a variety of legal and compliance requirements that must be met to operate legally and avoid potential legal problems. Entrepreneurs need to be familiar with the laws and regulations that apply to their businesses, including federal, state, and local laws.

Some of the critical legal and compliance considerations for businesses include:

- Business structure: Choosing the proper business structure, such as sole proprietorship, partnership, LLC, or corporation, that meets your needs and complies with the laws in your state. Each structure has its own set of legal and financial implications.
- Licenses and permits: Obtaining the necessary license and permits to operate your business. This can include business licenses, zoning permits, and professional licenses, depending on the nature of your business.
- Employment laws: Understanding and complying with federal and state laws related to issues such as minimum wage, overtime, equal opportunity, and anti-discrimination.
- Tax laws: Understanding and complying with federal

and state tax laws, including income taxes, sales taxes, and payroll taxes.
- Intellectual property: Protecting your business's intellectual property, such as trademarks, copyrights, and patents, and complying with laws related to their use.
- Contracts: Understanding and complying with the terms of agreements you enter into with customers, suppliers, and other businesses.
- Environmental and safety regulations: Understanding and complying with environmental protection and workplace safety regulations.

Entrepreneurs should consult an attorney and accountant to ensure their businesses comply with all applicable laws and regulations. They can also seek the guidance of industry trade groups and small business development centers for information on legal and compliance requirements.

This chapter discusses the importance of understanding and complying with legal compliance requirements when starting and running a business. We have also covered vital considerations, including business structure, licenses and permits, employment laws, tax laws, intellectual property, contracts, and environmental and safety regulations. In the next chapter, we will discuss the importance of financing and accounting for your business.

FINANCING AND ACCOUNTING

Proper financing and accounting practices are essential for the success of any business. Entrepreneurs need to have a clear understanding of their financial situation and be able to make informed decisions about how to allocate resources to achieve their goals.

Some of the critical finance and accounting considerations for businesses include:

- Capital: Obtaining the necessary money to start and grow your business, including personal savings, loans, investments from family and friends, or venture capital.
- Budgeting: Creating a budget for your business that outlines projected income and expenses and helps you to manage cash flow.
- Financial statements: Creating and maintaining accurate financial information, such as balance sheets, income statements, and cash flow statements, that provide a snapshot of your business's financial health.
- Taxation: Understanding and complying with federal and state tax laws, including income taxes, sales taxes, and payroll taxes.
- Record-keeping: Keeping accurate records of all financial

transactions and maintaining proper documentation, such as invoices, receipts, and bank statements.
- Auditing: Having an independent auditor review your financial statements to ensure they are accurate and compliant with accounting standards.

Entrepreneurs should consult with an accountant to ensure their financial practices are in order and get help with budgeting, financial statements, and tax compliance. They can also seek the guidance of small business development centers and industry trade groups for information on financing and accounting.

In this chapter, we have discussed the importance of clearly understanding your financial situation and making informed decisions about allocating resources to achieve your goals. We have also covered vital considerations, including capital, budgeting, financial statements, taxation, record-keeping, and auditing. In the next chapter, we will discuss the importance of sales and marketing for your business.

SALES AND MARKETING

Effective sales and marketing strategies are crucial for the success of any business. Entrepreneurs need to be able to attract and retain customers to generate revenue and grow their businesses.

Some of the critical sales and marketing considerations for businesses include:

- Market research: Understanding your target market, including demographics, needs, and preferences, to develop effective sales and marketing strategies.
- Product development: Developing products or services that meet the needs and preferences of your target market.
- Branding: Developing a strong brand that differentiates your business from the competition and helps to build customer loyalty.
- Pricing strategy: Setting competitive prices yet still allowing for a profit.
- Promotions and advertising: Develop and implement advertisements and advertising campaigns that reach your target market and effectively communicate the value of your products or services.
- Sales strategies: Developing and implementing effective

sales strategies, such as building a sales team, developing sales materials, and creating sales processes.
- Customer service: Providing excellent customer service to build customer loyalty and positive word-of-mouth.

Entrepreneurs should conduct market research and consult with marketing experts to develop effective sales and marketing strategies. They can also seek the guidance of small business development centers and industry trade groups for information on sales and marketing.

In this chapter, we have discussed the importance of effective sales and marketing strategies for the success of any business. We have also covered vital considerations, including market research, product development, branding, pricing strategy, promotions and advertising, sales strategies, and customer service. In the next chapter, we will discuss the importance of human resources for your business.

HUMAN RESOURCES AND ORGANIZATIONAL BEHAVIOR

Effective management of human resources and understanding organizational behavior are crucial for the success of any business. Entrepreneurs must attract and retain talented employees and create a positive work environment to drive productivity and growth.

Some of the vital human resources and organizational behavior considerations for businesses include:

- Recruitment and hiring: Attracting and selecting the best candidates for open positions in your company.
- Training and development: Providing your employees with the skills and knowledge they need to perform their jobs well.
- Performance management: Setting performance goals, providing feedback, and taking corrective action when necessary.

- Employee engagement: Keeping your employees motivated and committed to your company's goals.
- Communication: Developing effective communication channels and fostering an open and transparent work environment.
- Employee retention: Retaining your best employees by providing them with a positive work environment, opportunities for growth, and competitive compensation.
- Diversity and inclusion: Creating an inclusive and welcoming workplace for all employees, regardless of their background, identity or abilities.

Entrepreneurs should consult human resources experts and management consultants about developing effective HR policies and practices. They can also seek the guidance of small business development centers and industry trade groups for information on human resources and organizational behavior.

This chapter discusses the importance of effective human resources management and understanding organizational behavior for any business's success. We have also covered vital considerations, including recruitment and hiring, training and development, performance management, employee engagement, communication, employee retention, and diversity and inclusion. In the next chapter, we will discuss the importance of technology for your business.

TECHNOLOGY AND PRODUCTIVITY

Technology plays an increasingly important role in businesses of all sizes. To remain competitive and drive productivity and growth, entrepreneurs must stay up-to-date with the latest technologies.

Some of the vital technology and productivity considerations for businesses include:

- IT infrastructure: Ensuring your business has the hardware, software, and networking equipment to support your operations.
- Cybersecurity: Protect your business from cyber threats like hacking and data breaches.
- Automation: Implementing technology solutions that automate repetitive tasks and increase efficiency.
- Cloud computing: Utilizing cloud-based services to store and access data and applications remotely.
- Digital marketing: Utilizing digital channels to reach and engage with customers.
- Data analytics: Using data to make informed business decisions.
- Virtual and remote work: Utilizing technology to enable remote work and collaboration.

Entrepreneurs should consult with technology experts and consultants to develop effective technology strategies and implement the appropriate technology solutions. They can also seek the guidance of small business development centers and industry trade groups for information on technology and productivity.

In this chapter, we have discussed the importance of technology for the success of any business. We have also covered vital considerations, including IT infrastructure, cybersecurity, automation, cloud computing, digital marketing, data analytics, and virtual and remote work. In the next chapter, we will discuss the importance of financial management for your business.

FINANCIAL MANAGEMENT

Effective financial management is crucial for the success of any business. Entrepreneurs need to be able to create and manage budgets, track expenses, and make informed financial decisions to drive profitability and growth.

Some of the key financial management considerations for businesses include:

- Budgeting: Creating and managing a budget for your business to ensure you stay on track financially.
- Expense tracking: Keeping accurate records of all expenses to ensure that you stay within your budget and make informed financial decisions.
- Financial forecasting: Projecting future revenue and expenses to help plan for the future growth of your business.
- Financial analysis: Analyzing economic data to identify trends and make informed business decisions.
- Tax planning: Planning for taxes to minimize the impact of taxes on your business.
- Cash flow management: Managing cash flow to ensure your business has enough money to meet its obligations.
- Risk management: Identifying and managing financial

risks to minimize the potential negative impact on your business.

Entrepreneurs should consult financial experts and consultants about developing effective financial management strategies and implementing appropriate solutions. They can also seek the guidance of small business development centers and industry trade groups for information on financial management.

In this chapter, we have discussed the importance of effective financial management for the success of any business. We have also covered vital considerations, including budgeting, expense tracking, financial forecasting, financial analysis, tax planning, cash flow management, and risk management. In the next chapter, we will discuss the importance of sales and promotion for your business.

SALES AND PROMOTION

Effective sales and promotion strategies are crucial for revenue and growth for any business. Entrepreneurs need to be able to attract and retain customers and communicate the value of their products or services to succeed in today's competitive marketplace.

Some of the critical sales and promotion considerations for businesses include:

- Market research: Understanding the needs and wants of your target market to develop effective sales and promotion strategies.
- Product development: Developing products or services that meet the needs of your target market.
- Pricing strategy: Setting prices that are competitive and maximizing profitability.
- Sales techniques: Developing and implementing effective sales techniques to increase sales.
- Advertising and marketing: Utilizing advertising and marketing to reach and engage with potential customers.
- Public relations: Building and maintaining a positive public image for your business.

- Customer service: Providing excellent customer service to attract and retain customers.

Entrepreneurs should consult with sales and marketing experts and consultants to develop effective sales and promotion strategies and implement the appropriate solutions. They can also seek the guidance of small business development centers and industry trade groups for information on sales and promotion.

In this chapter, we have discussed the importance of sales and promotion for the success of any business. We have also covered vital considerations, including market research, product development, pricing strategy, sales techniques, advertising and marketing, public relations, and customer service. The next chapter discusses the importance of building and maintaining a solid team for your business.

BUILDING AND MAINTAINING A STRONG TEAM

Having a solid team in place is crucial for the success of any business. Entrepreneurs need to be able to attract, retain and motivate top talent to drive productivity, growth, and profitability.

Some of the critical considerations for building and maintaining a solid team include the following:

- Recruiting: Attracting and hiring top talent for your business.
- Training and development: Providing your team with the necessary training and development to perform their job effectively.
- Employee engagement: Creating a culture and environment that fosters employee engagement and satisfaction.
- Communication: Encouraging open and effective communication within your team.
- Performance management: Establishing a performance management system that allows you to track and

improve team performance.
- Employee retention: Implementing policies and practices that help to retain top talent within your organization.
- Organizational behavior: Understanding and managing the behavior of individuals and groups within your organization.

Entrepreneurs should consult with human resources experts and consultants to develop effective strategies for building and maintaining a solid team. They can also seek the guidance of small business development centers and industry trade groups for information on building and maintaining a solid team.

In this chapter, we have discussed the importance of building and maintaining a solid team for the success of any business. We have also covered vital considerations, including recruiting, training and development, employee engagement, communication, performance management, employee retention, and organizational behavior. In conclusion, we will summarize the key takeaways from this handbook and provide additional resources for entrepreneurs looking to open and grow their businesses.

ENVIRONMENTAL SUSTAINABILITY

In today's business landscape, it is essential to consider your operations' impact on the environment. Consumers, investors, and regulators are all paying increasing attention to the environmental impact of companies. As a business owner, it is vital to understand how to operate environmentally responsibly.

There are many ways to integrate environmental sustainability into your business operations, and this chapter will explore some of the most effective and practical approaches. Some of the critical topics that are to be covered include:By the end of this chapter, you will better understand how to operate your business in an environmentally responsible way and be equipped with the tools and knowledge to impact the environment while growing your business positively.

- The business case for environmental sustainability:

why it makes sense from both a financial and ethical standpoint
- Strategies for reducing the environmental impact of your operations, including energy efficiency, waste reduction, and sustainable sourcing
- How to communicate your environmental commitments to stakeholders and demonstrate your progress
- The legal and regulatory requirements for environmental compliance and how to ensure that your business is in compliance
- Best practices for incorporating environmental considerations into decision-making processes and operations

CONCLUSION

Opening and running a successful business requires knowledge, skill, and determination. This handbook has provided an overview of key considerations and strategies for entrepreneurs looking to open and grow their businesses, including creating a business plan, obtaining funding, managing finances, marketing and sales, and building and maintaining a solid team.

By following the guidance in this handbook, entrepreneurs will be well on their way to creating a successful and sustainable business. However, it is essential to note that this handbook needs to be completed and that there are many other resources and considerations that entrepreneurs should be aware of.

Some additional resources for entrepreneurs include:

- Small Business Development Centers (SBDCs) provide assistance and counseling to small business owners and entrepreneurs.
- SCORE: This organization provides free mentoring and counseling to small business owners and entrepreneurs.

- Industry trade groups: Joining industry trade groups can provide access to valuable resources, networking opportunities, and industry insights.

It's also important to remember that starting and growing a business requires continuous learning and improvements. Business owners should always be ready to adapt, adjust and learn new things that might arise.

In conclusion, this handbook has provided valuable information and guidance for entrepreneurs looking to open and grow their businesses. We wish you all the best in your entrepreneurial journey.

This handbook is not meant to be a substitute for professional advice and guidance but a starting point for entrepreneurs looking to open and grow their businesses. We encourage entrepreneurs to seek additional resources and guidance as they open and grow their businesses.

This handbook will be a valuable resource for entrepreneurs as they embark on starting and growing their businesses. Good luck, and may your business be successful!

GLOSSARY:

1. Business Plan: A document that outlines a business's goals, strategies, and financial projections.
2. Cash Flow: The amount of cash entering and going out of a business.
3. Entrepreneur: An individual who starts and manages a business.
4. Financial Projections: A forecast of a business's financial performance, including revenue, expenses, and profits.
5. Marketing: The process of promoting and selling products or services.
6. Organizational Behavior: The study of how people behave within an organization.
7. Productivity: The effectiveness and efficiency of a business in producing goods or services.
8. Sales: The process of selling products or services.
9. Startup: A new business venture.
10. SWOT Analysis: A method of evaluating a business's strengths, weaknesses, opportunities, and threats.
11. Target Market: The group of consumers a business is trying to reach.
12. Value Proposition: A statement that explains the unique value a business offers to its customers.
13. Venture Capital: Money provided by investors to finance a new business venture.
14. Business Model: The way a business creates, delivers, and captures value.

15. Branding: The practice of creating a name, symbol, or design that identifies and differentiates a product from other products.

REFERENCES:

1. "The Lean Startup" by Eric Ries
2. "Good to Great" by Jim Collins
3. "The E-Myth Revisited" by Michael Gerber
4. "Start with Why" by Simon Sinek
5. "The 7 Habits of Highly Effective People" by Stephen Covey
6. "The Power of Positive Thinking" by Norman Vincent Peale
7. "The Art of War" by Sun Tzu
8. "The 4-Hour Work Week" by Timothy Ferriss
9. "Influence: The Psychology of Persuasion" by Robert Cialdini
10. "The Business Model Generation" by Alexander Osterwalder and Yves Pigneur

These books provide a wealth of knowledge and insights on various aspects of starting and growing a business, from developing a business plan and creating a value proposition to managing cash flow and increase productivity. They offer practical advice and strategies for entrepreneurs and are a valuable resource for anyone looking to start or grow a business.

SAMPLE BUSINESS PLAN

Executive Summary:

Green Cleaners is a new business that will provide eco-friendly and sustainable dry cleaning services to the local community. We will use environmentally safe cleaning products and processes to clean clothes and other textiles while reducing our carbon footprint and promoting sustainability. Our target market will be individuals and households in the local area looking for a cleaner and greener alternative to traditional dry cleaning services.

Business Description:

Green Cleaners will be a full-service dry cleaning business providing our customers with a wide range of services.

1. We will clean and press clothes and other textiles such as curtains, bedding, and tablecloths.
2. We will also offer alterations, repairs, and laundry services for items that can't be dry-cleaned.
3. We will have an online ordering system and provide free pick-up and delivery services for our customers' convenience.

Market Analysis:

The dry cleaning industry has seen steady growth in recent years and is expected to continue to grow. However, the industry is also becoming increasingly competitive. To differentiate ourselves from our competitors, we will focus on providing eco-friendly and sustainable services that appeal to environmentally conscious consumers. We will also focus on providing excellent customer service with an online ordering system, free pick-up and delivery services, and quick turnaround times.

Marketing and Sales:

Green Cleaners will use a variety of marketing tactics to reach our target market. We will use social media and online advertising to reach a wider audience and targeted marketing campaigns to reach environmentally conscious consumers. We will also offer special promotions and discounts to attract new customers. Additionally, we will build relationships with local businesses and organizations, such as providing special rates for bulk cleaning services.

Operations and Management:

Green Cleaners will be owned and operated by John Smith, who has over ten years of experience in the dry cleaning industry. John will be responsible for the overall operations and management of the business and will hire additional staff as needed. We will use eco-friendly and sustainable cleaning products and processes to clean clothes and other textiles. We will also have a modern online ordering system and offer free pick-up and delivery services for our customers' convenience.

Financial Projections:

We expect Green Cleaners to break even within the first year of operations and to achieve profitability by the end of the second year. Our projected revenue for the first year is $250,000, with projected expenses of $230,000. Our projected revenue for the second year is $300,000, with projected costs of $280,000. We will use the profits generated to expand the business, including opening additional locations in the future.

Conclusion:

Green Cleaners will provide eco-friendly and sustainable dry cleaning services to the local community while reducing our carbon footprint and promoting sustainability. We will differentiate ourselves from competitors by providing excellent customer service and using eco-friendly and sustainable cleaning products and processes. We expect to achieve profitability within the first two years of operations and will use the profits generated to expand the business.

SAMPLE INTERVIEW PLAN

Interview Plan for Employers

Introduction:

This interview plan aims to provide a structured and consistent approach to interviewing candidates for open positions at our company. The project includes a list of critical questions to ask during the interview and a set of evaluation criteria for assessing the candidate's qualifications and fit for the role.

Preparation:

Before the interview, the hiring manager or HR representative should review the job description and requirements for the open position and the candidate's resume and application materials. They should also prepare a list of specific questions to help them assess the candidate's qualifications and fit for the role.

Conducting the Interview:

The interview should begin with a brief introduction and overview of the company and the open position. The interviewer should then ask open-ended questions to encourage candidates to discuss their qualifications, experience, and skills. Some sample questions include:

- Can you tell me about your previous experience in this field?
- How do you handle challenges and difficult situations in the workplace?
- How do you stay organized and manage your time effectively?
- Can you give an example of a successful project you have completed in the past?
- How do you work with and communicate effectively with colleagues and team members?

The interviewer should also ask the candidate about their goals and career aspirations and how they see the open position fitting into their long-term career plans.

Evaluation:

After the interview, the hiring manager or HR representative should use the following evaluation criteria to assess the candidate's qualifications and fit for the role:

- **Experience and qualifications:** Does the candidate have the appropriate knowledge and qualifications for the position?
- **Skills and abilities:** Does the candidate have the skills and abilities required for the job?
- **Fit and compatibility:** Does the candidate fit the company culture and team well?
- **Career aspirations:** Does the candidate's career aspirations align with the company's goals and plans for the role?

The hiring manager or HR representative should also consider any red flags that may have come up during the interview, such as lack of experience or poor communication skills.

Conclusion:

By following this interview plan, employers will be able to conduct structured and consistent interviews that will help them assess the qualifications and fit of candidates for open positions. This will help ensure that the best candidates are selected for the role and that they will be a good fit for the company and the team.

SAMPLE INTERVIEW

Questions for Employers

1. Can you tell me about your previous experience in this field?
2. How do you handle challenges and difficult situations in the workplace?
3. How do you stay organized and manage your time effectively?
4. Can you give an example of a successful project you have completed in the past?
5. How do you work with and communicate effectively with colleagues and team members?
6. Can you explain a situation where you had to think strategically and how you approached it?
7. How do you keep up to date with the latest trends and developments in this industry?
8. How do you prioritize tasks and meet deadlines?
9. Can you tell me about a time when you had to make a difficult decision?
10. How do you handle constructive feedback and criticism?
11. How do you approach problem-solving and decision-making?
12. Can you tell me about a situation where you had to adapt to a change in the workplace?
13. How do you handle stress and pressure in the workplace?

14. How do you manage and lead a team effectively?
15. Can you give an example of a time when you had to collaborate with a diverse group of people?
16. What was a time when you had to make a presentation or pitch?
17. How do you handle conflicts and disagreements with colleagues or team members?
18. How do you approach to feedback and coaching for your team members?
19. What is a situation where you had to take the initiative and lead a project?
20. How do you measure your performance and set goals for yourself?

TIPS FOR GIVING POSITIVE REINFORCEMENTS:

1. Be specific: When giving positive feedback, identify the particular behavior or action you are praising.
2. Be timely: Give positive feedback as soon as possible after the event or behavior occurs; this will help to reinforce the desired behavior.
3. Be sincere in your praise, and avoid using overly formal or insincere language.
4. Be consistent: Regularly give positive feedback to employees to help them maintain positive behaviors and attitudes.
5. Use various reinforcement methods: Reinforcements can take many forms, such as verbal praise, bonuses, and promotions. Using a variety of ways can help to keep employees motivated and engaged.

TIPS FOR GIVING NEGATIVE REINFORCEMENTS:

1. Be specific: As with positive feedback, identify the particular behavior or action that needs improvement.
2. Be timely: Address negative behaviors or actions as soon as possible so the employee can make necessary changes.
3. Be objective: Avoid using subjective language or making personal attacks. Stick to the facts and focus on the behavior or action that needs improvement.
4. Be constructive: Provide specific suggestions for how the employee can improve and offer support to help them make changes.
5. Follow-up: After giving negative feedback, the follow-up is to see if the employee has made any improvements and provide positive feedback when they do.

STEP-BY-STEP GUIDE TO OPENING A BUSINESS:

1. Develop a business plan: This should include a detailed description of your business, your target market, financial projections, and a marketing strategy.
2. Conduct market research: Research your market to understand your target customers and the competition.
3. Register your business: Register with the appropriate state and local authorities, and obtain any necessary licenses or permits.
4. Obtain funding: Look into various funding options, such as loans, grants, or investors, to help finance your business.
5. Choose a location: Look for a suitable place for your business, keeping in mind factors such as accessibility, visibility, and zoning laws.
6. Hire staff: Recruit and hire staff to help run your business, including managers, employees, and freelancers.
7. Establish accounting and legal systems: Set up accounting and legal systems to ensure that your business complies with all relevant laws and

regulations.
8. Create a marketing plan: Develop a marketing plan to promote your business and attract customers.
9. Launch your business: Once all preparations have been made, launch your business to the public.
10. Continuously monitor and evaluate your progress: Monitor and assess your progress, make adjustments if necessary and maintain good relationships with your staff and customers.

SOURCES OF FUNDING FOR BUSINESS.

1. Personal savings: You can use your savings to fund your business or ask friends or family to invest in it.
2. Small Business Administration (SBA) loans: The SBA provides loans to small businesses through participating lenders.
3. Bank loans: Banks offer loans to small businesses, including term loans, lines of credit, and SBA-guaranteed loans.
4. Venture capital: Venture capitalists provide funding to businesses with high growth potential in exchange for equity in the company.
5. Angel investors: Angel investors are high-net-worth individuals who provide funding to businesses in exchange for equity.
6. Crowdfunding: Platforms like Kickstarter and Indiegogo allow individuals to contribute money to a business in exchange for rewards or equity.
7. Grants: Some governments, non-profit organizations, and other entities assist small businesses for specific purposes, such as research and development or particular industries.
8. Microfinance organizations: Microfinance organizations provide small loans to entrepreneurs and small business

owners in developing countries.

It is important to note that each funding source has its requirements and qualifications, and it's essential to carefully consider the terms and conditions of any funding before accepting it.

QUIZ:

1. What are the three primary components of a business plan? a) Executive summary, marketing plan, financial projections b) Operations plan, management team, product or service c) Vision statement, mission statement, company history d) All of the above
2. Which of the following is not a common funding source for small businesses? a) Bank loans b) Crowdfunding c) Personal savings d) Stock market investments
3. When motivating staff, which of the following is not a suitable method? a) Providing positive reinforcement b) Job enrichment c) Ignoring their contributions d) All are suitable methods
4. What is the Small Business Administration (SBA)? a) A government agency that provides funding to small businesses b) A private organization that offers small business consulting services c) A non-profit organization that provides grants to small businesses d) A network of business owners that provide mentorship and support
5. What are the benefits of creating excellent organizational behavior for the business? a) Increased productivity and job satisfaction b) Improved communication and decision-making c) Greater employee engagement d) All of the above

ANSWERS:

1. (b) Operations plan, management team, product or service
2. (d) Stock market investments
3. (c) Ignoring their contributions
4. (a) A government agency that provides funding to small businesses
5. (d) All of the above

EPILOGUE

Starting and growing a business is a journey that requires dedication, hard work, and perseverance. We hope this handbook has provided valuable information and insights to help entrepreneurs at all stages of the business-building process.

As you work to open and grow your business, remember to stay true to your vision and values, to stay informed and adaptable, to seek out help and resources, and to acknowledge and appreciate your successes along the way.

Starting a business is a challenging task, but it can be gratifying. Building a business is a journey that will help you grow as a person and as a professional, and it will be a source of pride and accomplishment for you.

We hope this handbook has provided a helpful guide on opening and running a business. Remember, the most

important thing is to enjoy the process and never give up on your dream. Entrepreneurship is an exciting and challenging journey, and we wish you all the best as you embark on it.

We hope that you found this handbook helpful and informative.

We wish you success on your entrepreneurial journey.

AFTERWORD

Starting and growing a business is a challenging and rewarding journey. It requires passion, skill, and determination to turn an idea into a successful enterprise. We hope this handbook has provided valuable information and insights for entrepreneurs at all stages of the business-building process.

Building a successful business takes time and effort, and it's essential to keep focused on your goals and be persistent in facing challenges.

It's also important to stay updated on the latest trends and developments in your industry. The business world is constantly evolving, and staying informed and adaptable will help you stay ahead of the curve.

In addition, feel free to ask for help and seek out resources and guidance as you navigate the process of opening and growing your business. Countless organizations, resources, and individuals can provide valuable support and advice.

Finally, remember to celebrate your successes and reflect on the lessons you've learned. Starting and growing a business is a challenging but rewarding journey, and it's essential to acknowledge and appreciate your progress.

We wish you all the best as you continue on your entrepreneurial journey. May your business be successful!

ACKNOWLEDGEMENT

We want to express our deepest gratitude to all those who have helped and supported us in creating this handbook.

Firstly, we would like to thank our families and friends for their unwavering support and encouragement throughout the writing process. Their love and understanding have been invaluable sources of inspiration and motivation.

We would also like to thank our colleagues and mentors who have provided valuable guidance and feedback on the content of this handbook. Their expertise and experience have helped to make this handbook a valuable resource for entrepreneurs.

We would also like to acknowledge the countless business owners and entrepreneurs whose stories and experiences inspired this handbook. Their willingness to share their knowledge and insights have contributed to the content of this handbook.

Finally, we thank our readers for their interest in this handbook. We hope that it will be a useful resource for entrepreneurs at all stages of the business-building process.

Thank you all.

Disclaimer:

The information provided in this book is for general informational purposes only. It is not intended as professional business advice and should not be relied upon as such. The author and publisher make no representations or warranties of any kind, express or implied, about the completeness, accuracy, reliability or suitability of the information contained in this book. Any reliance you place on such information is strictly at your own risk. The author and publisher will not be liable for any errors, omissions, or any damages arising from the use of the information contained in this book. The reader should always seek professional advice before making business or financial decisions.

ABOUT THE AUTHOR

Norris Elliott

Norris Elliott is a successful entrepreneur with over 15 years of experience in the industry. He has started and grown several successful small businesses in various sectors and has a wealth of knowledge and experience to share with others. Norris is passionate about helping entrepreneurs and small business owners succeed. He has dedicated his career to providing valuable guidance and resources to those looking to start or grow a business. In addition to his business experience, Norris holds an BSC in Construction Engineering and Management from University of Technology, Jamaica and has been mentoring several small business owners. Norris resides inKingston City with his family and continues to consult and advise entrepreneurs and small business owners. He is also working on his next book, focusing on scaling a business.

BOOKS BY THIS AUTHOR

Wealth By Design: How To Build A Life Of Financial Freedom

"Financial Literacy and Wealth Building: A Comprehensive Guide" is essential for anyone looking to take control of their financial future. Written by author Ellionaire, this book covers everything you need to know about building wealth and achieving financial freedom, including understanding financial basics, creating a budget, investing, and planning for the future. With real-world examples and practical tips, this book is a must-have for anyone looking to improve their financial literacy and achieve financial success. Whether a beginner or an experienced investor, this book will provide you with the knowledge and tools you need to reach your financial goals. With easy-to-understand language and a step-by-step approach, "Financial Literacy and Wealth Building" is the perfect guide for anyone looking to take control of their finances and build a better future.

"The Great Easter Egg Hunt"

"The Great Easter Egg Hunt" is a children's book that tells the story of a small village where the annual Easter egg hunt is about to take place. However, this year there's a twist. The eggs have been hidden by a mischievous Easter Bunny named Benny, who has added a few challenges to the hunt.

"The Jellybean Journey,"

In "The Jellybean Journey," a group of friends embark on a quest to find the mythical Jellybean Tree. They journey through various terrains, including deserts, mountains, and forests, and encounter a variety of creatures and obstacles along the way.

The Children's Bible: Uncovering The Wonders Of God's Word

In "The Jellybean Journey," a group of friends embark on a quest to find the mythical Jellybean Tree. They journey through various terrains, including deserts, mountains, and forests, and encounter a variety of creatures and obstacles along the way.

"The Great Jellybean Adventure"

"The Great Jellybean Adventure" is a story about a group of jellybeans who discover a mysterious portal and embark on a wild journey to see where it leads. Along the way, they face all sorts of obstacles and challenges, but they never give up and use their creativity and teamwork to overcome them.

"The Mouse In The House To Play"

"The Mouse in the House To Play" is an exciting and heartwarming adventure story for children. It follows the journey of Tim and Amy, two siblings who are home alone while their parents are on a trip. They are bored and have nothing to do until they hear a noise in the house. They investigate and find a tiny mouse named Mickey who has found his way into the home.

Notes

Notes

Notes

Notes

Notes

Notes

Made in the USA
Columbia, SC
11 July 2025